Letters to Emma

John Ostdiek, OFM

Published by Romeii Media Group
PO Box 486, Hudson, WI 54016
romeii.com

Printed in the United States of America 2023 - 1st Edition

Library of Congress Cataloging-in-Publications Data
Letters to Emma
ISBN-13 978-1-937391-83-6
1. John 2. Ostdiek, OFM

2023

TABLE OF CONTENTS

DEDICATION

For Emma and future generations

LETTER 1

Introduction

This starts a series of "letters" to help Emma and all young people to get a grasp of the happenings in my lifetime. The seed for these letters sprouted at the 2015 OJJ (Ostdiek Jubilee Jamboree). Emma, your mother Sara and your grandmother Annette asked me to hold you, a seven-month-old baby at the time, for photos. Cameras clicked, you laughed.

Then an unspoken question popped into my mind, *"Emma, suppose that the calendar reads 2100. You are 85 years old. What sort of life have you experienced?"*

Your expected answer troubles me. Why? I see "dark clouds" on our country's horizon. They can threaten you and your fellow citizens with serious problems. I hope and pray that you can weather them gracefully.

To help you, I suggest a "lesson" for your consideration in each of the following letters.

Best! Bless!
John

LETTER 2

My Background, Briefly

Dear Emma,

At this writing in November 2022, I have reached the age of 100. Many happenings stand out in my own memory. In the following letters I offer you a quick incident-by-incident summary and draw a "lesson" from each. But first a summary of my life:

Aug. 27, 1922: Born. Eldest of 5 boys and 5 girls born to Henry and Dora Ostdiek. All born on a farm near Lawrence, Nebraska.

1936: Graduated from St. Stephen's School near Lawrence.

1936-1942: Studied high school and junior college at St. Joseph Minor Seminary, Westmont, Illinois. The imported "gymnasium" system.

1942-1943: Franciscan novitiate at Teutopolis, Illinois.

1943-1945: Philosophy study, Our Lady of Angels Seminary, Cleveland, Ohio.

1945-1949: Theology studies, St. Joseph Seminary, Teutopolis, Illinois.

June 24, 1949: Ordained priest, Teutopolis, Illinois.

1949-1950: Homiletic and biology undergrad at Quincy University.

1950-1953: Teacher of high school biology at St. Joseph Seminary.

1953-1954: Completion of undergrad biology at Creighton University, Omaha, Nebraska.

1954-1960: MS and PhD studies, Catholic University, Washington, DC, and auxiliary Catholic chaplain at Walter Reed Army Hospital in Washington, DC.

1960- 1983: Professor of biology at Quincy University and Mundelein, Chicago, Illinois.

1983-present: Retreat and itinerant preaching, hospital chaplain, various boards, writer of more than 400 articles. Retired.

Love,
John

LETTER 3

A Dime For a Bushel of Corn

Dear Emma,

Yes, *"A dime for a bushel of corn,"* stands out in my memory as a good description of the Great Depression in 1930. Unimaginable today! But... it happened, even to me at age 8.

The event: I was in the kitchen doing some "little boy" thing, when Dad entered and told Mom that he had just returned from selling a load of corn at the market elevator in Lawrence for *"a dime for a bushel."* In those days, a "load" meant 50 bushels, the content capacity of the horse-drawn wagon. And a "dime" was 10 cents then as it is today. That's my description of the Great Depression... ugh!

After that sale, Dad changed our farm's operations. Instead of selling grain, he fed it to about a dozen milk cows, and sold cream each week to a nearby creamery, which made butter. A second change: increasing the flock of hens for selling eggs by the case. Both added hours to the workloads of family members.

The lesson? I like Abe Lincoln's way of phrasing it: *"If you can't plow through it, plow around it."* Abe made good sense then and now.

Love,
John

LETTER 4

A Very Bad Dust Storm Threatens a Baby's Life

Dear Emma,

A Dust Bowl storm threatened a baby's life one night in early April 1935. The Dust Bowl occurred in the late winters and springs of the years 1934-1940, when ground-level clouds roared at speeds of around 50 mph, carrying tons of very fine dust many miles in through the Midwest High Plains area of the U.S, from Texas to the Canadian border.

One of the worst dust storms hit south central Nebraska and our family farm that April evening. Our family gathered, as a cloud of very fine dust formed in my parents' bedroom. One-month-old baby Fritz cried and choked. Mom did all she could, but nothing quieted him.

Finally, she placed the baby in a large shoe box, built an arch over it, then covered it with wet towels and placed all in a closet. That quieted the baby.

At age 12, I just stood there, in fear, watching a mother fight for her baby's life. SHE WON!

Until Mom died in 1996, we family members saw a special mother-son relationship in action. Her reply to suggestions we made: *"I'll talk it over with Fritz."*

What a lesson! Often, we bypassed her by talking with Fritz before presenting our concern to her.

Love,
John

LETTER 5

Rains! Flood of the Republican River

Dear Emma,

May 1935. Strange, but in a drought year, southern Nebraska had rains for 14 days during May. Talk was that maybe the drought was ending? Instead, a flood tore through the two-mile-wide valley of the Republican River. As I recall, run-off water from rainstorms washed out a dam in the river's western section (eastern Colorado, northwestern Kansas). Result? Wild, churning, dirty water, wreaking havoc on everything in its path.

My Dad, ever interested in the "unusual," invited me to go with him to see this flood closeup, standing on a riverbank near Red Cloud, Nebraska. His words, *"You may never have another chance to see a flood like this."*

Sight? You bet! A whole haystack floating by, and the Burlington Railroad's track twisted, poking up for 10 feet in the air. Pieces of barns, houses, outbuildings—debris and more debris!

That day I saw a raw, very raw, disaster, huge and unforgiving! Claiming plant and animal life, a ruined river valley, human work floating downstream! Gone!

What a lesson for me!

Love,
John

LETTER 6

Hailstorm Defeats Dad

Dear Emma,

Mid-June 1935. I remember the weather started as a cloudy but nice day. Dad and I seeded cane in a small field that afternoon, a job we wanted to finish before the wheat harvest that was right ahead of us. But the clouds had built up and then rumbled; their way of telling us that "Hail is next!" We hurried home and got safely into the house, just before the blast of hailstones hit our farm.

It was one of the worst hailstorms I ever experienced. All of us just stood by the house windows, watching hailstones hit the ground and roll to the fence of the yard, building a foot of ice. It demolished the wheat crop, just before harvest.

Dad couldn't take it. He left window-watching, went to his bedroom, threw himself on his bed, and started sobbing. Me? Dumbstruck. For the first—and only—time in his life, had I ever seen Dad truly and completely "beat."

Later in the evening, he recovered. He went to the pump organ in the living room and started playing songs. Quickly, we kids gathered around him, and began singing as he played. And SING we did! For an hour. Song became our recovery. Do it **together**. That, too, stands out strongly as a lesson.

Love,
John

LETTER 7

The Cowboy Herding Cattle

Dear Emma,

During the Dust Bowl years, we made every attempt to find enough grass for grazing cows. We even used some nearby unfenced grassland. So, I had to herd them. Literally, a real cowboy. Not very difficult. In fact, boring at times. I snapped sitting grasshoppers with my long, leather cord whip and I got fairly good at doing so.

I learned a lot by herding cattle. They stay near each other while grazing. When it was time to drive them back to the home corral, I called my dog, Shep, to help. He knew the correct road to the home corral and kept the cows walking toward it. They knew what his barks meant. A herd of cattle has a definite pecking order. The last cow in the line was always the same one. Shep stayed right behind her, just beyond the reach of her hind hoof kick, a hard one.

One day, her kick paid off. An unsuspecting jack rabbit sauntered right behind her. WHAM! Dead rabbit! That night we enjoyed nice fried rabbit for supper. Shep feasted on the scraps and bones.

Lesson: Mother Nature is a smart lady who can teach us a lot.

Love,
John

LETTER 8

A Glimpse of Lawrence, Nebraska

Dear Emma,

As we leave childhood stories, I want to share a quick look at my hometown, Lawrence, located in south central Nebraska near Kansas. Population: About 400, in 1930, and about 200 in 2000 A.D.

The town and area were first settled in the 1870s, mainly by German and Bohemian immigrants. Most were Catholics. Nearly all Native Americans had died from "white people's" diseases, through contact with Oregon Trail and Civil War travelers in the 1850s and 1860s.

The people of Lawrence were hardworking, family-oriented, loved to dance and play cards, helpful to neighbors, thankful to escape crowded Europe, willing to help the few sickly Native Americans still there, and steady Catholics. In short, successful.

The Dust Bowl years, from 1934-1940, had a drastic effect on the people of Lawrence. Over one-half lost ownership of their farms. My parents rented, not owned, a farm, and struggled to raise 10 children. Only Mildred stayed. The rest of us found other places to work and live. But all still love that "L"!

Lesson: We learned to work through tough times and sing a song in the evening.

Love,
John

LETTER 9

Franciscan Minor Seminary

In May 1936, I graduated from St. Stephen's District 5 Public Grade School. I shared academic first place honors with another Nuckoll County student that year. Chapter ended…then what?

I had two strong "likes" for future careers: medicine and priesthood. I chose the priesthood because my uncle, Brother Art Rempe, OFM, served on the support staff of the Franciscan St. Joseph Minor Seminary in Westmont, Illinois, near Chicago. Simply put, I wanted to be with him. I had never met a Franciscan priest before entering their seminary.

I shared my hopes with Mom and Dad. They approved. Many years later, Mom told me that she and Dad had needed me at home but also wanted me to be a priest if I truly wanted to do so. Gaining acceptance? It had us laughing. I had mailed my application early in the summer of 1936. Waited and waited. No reply. When it arrived at last (whew!), it contained only a strip-tape with the number "1" repeated in all its length. What? Mom laughed when I showed it to her. She ventured that this was my laundry number for washable clothes, and that meant I was accepted. Right guess, Mom! I entered the seminary in September 1936.

Lesson: Choose what fits you.

Love,
John

LETTER 10

Minor Seminary Years

I spent six school years (1936-1942) at St. Joseph Seminary, Westmont, Illinois, boarding in high school and junior college seminary in the European "gymnasium" pattern. Languages: Latin, Greek, German, and English as the backbone for philosophy and theology. My favorite? English writing. Our curriculum also included physics, history, math, and speech, with a side of band and choral music. Athletics, if you liked. I played outfield on the baseball varsity. Long throwing arm.

One course stands out in my memory: first-year college history, 1940-1941. World War II had Europe in flames. The professor offered to lecture on this present-day (at the time) war day-by-day, instead of studying the history of the late 19th to early 20th centuries. We students clapped! It was one of the best courses I had during seminary years.

During the 1940s, the U.S. drafted young men for military service but exempted seminarians. Why? The military could draft enough soldiers and sailors but lacked enough chaplains. So, they prescribed that we seminarians restrict our studies to basic necessities. Our Franciscans reduced philosophy to two years instead of three.

Lesson: Strike for a balance in life. Mine? Hospital chaplain during master's and doctoral studies and research.

Love,
John

LETTER 11

The Doubting Thomas Scientist

Dear Emma,

Many of us can pinpoint some event/occasion/person in our lives that brought about a significant change in the direction of our life's path. Here's mine:

At the conclusion of my third year of high school at St. Joseph Seminary, I packed my bags and headed for home in Nebraska—a *long* bus ride from Chicago in that early June of 1939. I had decided to discontinue studies for the priesthood but was unclear as to what to do next.

It just so happened that my seatmate on this trip was a young scientist from the Smithsonian Institution in Washington, DC. He intended to spend some of the summer studying the extinct large elephant-like animal remains housed in the museum at the University of Nebraska in Lincoln. That struck my fancy! We talked a lot.

Sometime during that discussion, religion became the subject. He doubted that God existed. "Strange… very strange!" I thought. Why was he so unsure? I don't remember if we argued the issue or not. But we did talk about it. Then, later in the evening as we traveled through western Iowa approaching Omaha, with a sky gloriously lighted by the setting sun, he remarked, "When you see a sunset like this, you think that only God could do so."

That did it! Clearly my future! To be a spokesperson to those undecided—especially scientists—about God's presence in our lives and world. No way then, of course, could I even imagine how this would gradually become real over the years! I stayed in the seminary, became a priest, a scientist, a professor, and a writer.

Now 87 years later, I can only say that God "called" me through a "Doubting Thomas" scientist. Thanks, God, for doing so!

Lesson: Sometimes God communicates through sunsets.

Love,
John

LETTER 12

Entering the Franciscan Novitiate

Dear Emma,

On August 9-10, 1942, I left the family home permanently to enter the Franciscan novitiate in Teutopolis, Illinois. We candidates numbered 35 young men.

During the official entrance ceremony on August 19, 1942, each of us candidates received the Franciscan "habit" and a new first name. From "Norbert Francis" I became "John Leonard" (Patron saint: Giovani Leonardi, Feast Day: October 9). Ever since, I have answered to "John." The name has stuck but the habit—a brown outer robe with a white cord as a belt—serves mostly when we dress formally.

In mid-November 1942, our uncle, Brother Art Rempe, OFM, came to the novitiate to pronounce his final vows. Knowing my relationship to Art, our Provincial, who was the celebrant for the ceremony, asked me to serve as master of ceremony. With a twinkling eye, he promised to move in the ceremony only when I asked him to do so. Believe me… I studied hard! All performed okay.

The novitiate ended on August 20, 1943, in the ceremony of pronouncing our vows. The next day we traveled to Our Lady of Angels Seminary in Cleveland, Ohio, for a two-year study of philosophy.

Lesson: Our life here on Earth serves as a long novitiate for Heaven.

Love,
John

LETTER 13

Two Years Studying Philosophy

Dear Emma,

Within a few days in late August 1943, we newly professed friars boarded a couple of school buses. Yes! Old-school pre-war buses. Thank God that they made a safe trip from Teutopolis, Illinois to Our Lady of Angels Seminary in Cleveland, Ohio.

Once there, we settled into two school years of studying courses in philosophy. In Latin, of course. Textbooks, professors' lectures, students' written exams—all in Latin. The thinking of those years placed philosophy as preparation for understanding theology. I got through but have no notes from those courses in my files.

And, because of World War II, visiting and shopping in the city became difficult. All soldiers and sailors were required to wear uniforms, even off duty. So, when in town, we seminarians had to wear the official clergy attire: black suit and Roman collar. Otherwise, we would be openly criticized.

Result? I have very few memories of the city of Cleveland. The daily grind of studying philosophy—in Latin, mind you—remains in the back shelf of my mind.

Lesson: Sometimes, we face unpleasantries in life.

Love,
John

LETTER 14

Four Years Studying Theology, 1945-1949

Dear Emma,

September 1945 found me back in Teutopolis, Illinois at St. Joseph Seminary as one of the 100 Franciscan students there for four years' study of theology, the prep for priesthood ministry after ordination. Again, these were the years just during and after WWII, and before the Vatican II Council of the world's Catholic bishops. Both events had major influence on study and life at the seminary.

The content of our study of theology came mostly from several centuries of European Catholic authors. Again, in Latin: books, lectures, questions, and exams. Somehow, for example, studying about sex (in Latin!) did not prepare us very well for hearing American confessions. Nor for preaching sermons to American grade schoolers.

A language incident from the mid-century, about 1950, reveals a lesson. A pastor requested a priest who could speak German to come to his parish and hear confessions of elderly people who had learned how to go to confession in German. I offered. Sure enough, a goodly number confessed in German. Among them, a grandmother-aged lady. I responded in German to her confession. She interrupted me, asking me to speak in English because she did not understand German!

Lesson: Sometimes, humor sneaks into a story. Have a laugh.

Love,
John

LETTER 15

Gardener on the Side

Dear Emma,

Yes, from the fall of 1943 until the spring of 1949, during study years after novitiate, I lived that title, *"Gardener on the side."* The study of philosophy and theology stood as most important during that time, but some form of "chores" occupied a second duty. Given my farmer background, gardening seemed a natural choice.

First, I worked and learned a lot under an upperclassman, Fr. Val. He came from a truck garden family and shared much of his skill in raising vegetables with me. Eventually, he passed the "boss" position to me.

Raising vegetables in 1945-1949 on a one-and-a-half-acre garden meant planting and tending 800 tomato plants and matching beds of celery, beans, carrots, beets, etc. Some six to eight other friar-students assisted me. To feed 100 friar students, faculty, and staff, took a bushel of tomatoes or other veggies each dinner.

During and after the war years, we got creative and used composting instead of commercial fertilizers. That attracted the attention of townsfolk. They complimented our fine yields. Our religious superiors also noticed our success. After my ordination, my farmer-gardener background led them to assign me to teach biology, even though I had no prior academic course in it during my seminary years.

Lesson? Find out your best skill. Develop it.

Love,
John

LETTER 16

Ordination to the Priesthood

Dear Emma,

On Friday, June 24, 1949, I reached a major life's goal: ordination as a Catholic priest. What a day! The exclamation point after 13 years of preparation. With my parents and siblings present as my personal guests, Bishop O'Connor of Springfield, Illinois, ordained 20 of us Franciscans in St. Francis Church, Teutopolis, Illinois.

On Wednesday, June 29, 1949, I celebrated my First Solemn Mass in St. Stephen Church, a mission church near Lawrence, Nebraska, the site of my babyhood baptism. Fr. Haskamp, pastor and friend, hosted me and many guests, including four Franciscans, cousin Fr. Frank Ostdiek from Des Moines, Iowa, a half dozen local priests, and a full church.

My entire family served in roles for that first Mass. Dad took his place on the organ bench to play and direct the choir. To this day, I still choke up when I recall his dedication. With her ever-present smile, Mom greeted guests. Mildred holding her baby, Joe, and Anita holding her baby, Marian. Sister Lenore in full nun's habit. Hank served as an usher. Gil and Fritz as altar servers. Jo the traditional "bride," and Lou, her attendant. Art as candle bearer. The entire family helping me celebrate! Thanks be to God!

Emma: How can you ever forget life's major moments? How can I?

Love!
John

LETTER 17

The Start of a New and Long Career

Dear Emma,

It's the end of summer, 1949. I'm packed and ready to move to Quincy College in Quincy, Illinois, for the mandatory year of study of homiletics. On the night before leaving the seminary, I visited the rector, Fr. Seraphin Tibesar, OFM, to offer thanks for the four years of theology studies. I also mentioned that I had no info on what ministry would follow the homiletic year. He offered, *"I know only that you are scheduled to teach at the minor seminary."* Good news!

A few days later, now at Quincy, I called the rector of the seminary, asking what plans he had for me. He replied, *"Teach biology! During this year at Quincy take some biology courses so that you meet Illinois' teaching standards."*

That started one of the busiest years of my life: Two semesters of homiletics, four courses in biology, three courses in education, one semester of part-time teaching high school religion, a virtual seminar on St. Bonaventure's writings, and a summer of chemistry. Whew!

But it had a nice ending: B.S. in education and qualified to teach high school biology and religion.

A double lesson: Sometimes, we must do more than usual. And sometimes, we may need to change directions.

Love,
John

LETTER 18

Graduate Studies with My Major Professor

Dear Emma,

After three years of teaching high school biology at the minor seminary, I asked to take a summer course in field biology at Creighton University in Omaha, Nebraska. While there, the Provincial surprised me by asking that I stay through the school year to complete undergraduate studies in biology. Good idea.

Then, in 1954, the Provincial asked me to transfer to Catholic University in Washington, DC, for master's degree graduate study in biology, beginning in September 1954. A second good idea.

Then, a third step. One day in early 1955, Dr. Herbert Hanson, my major professor at Catholic University, asked me, *"Do you want to go to Alaska for a research project?"* Certainly!

The U.S. Office of Naval Research wanted an ecological study of freshwater Alaskan blackfish found in northern Alaska. Sure! Sounds great for a master's thesis! A unique fish, living in ice during the winters, thaws out in the spring and feeds on mosquito larvae.

And finally, a fourth step! When the Provincial found out that the prominent Office of Naval Research had chosen and funded me under temporary rank of "commander" and approved my report, he asked me to continue studies for a doctorate, under the guidance of Dr. Hanson. Teaching at Quincy University would be my assignment, instead of the minor seminary.

Lesson: Accept good things. Make the most you can with them.

Love,
John

LETTER 19

In Alaska to Study Alaskan Blackfish

Dear Emma,

Late May 1955, I flew (via military plane) to Point Barrow, Alaska, the home base for ecological study of the Alaskan blackfish, found in the freshwaters of the northernmost areas of Alaska. The mission? A study requested and funded by the Office of Naval Research.

A unique fish! It survives living in the winter's freshwater ice to feed on mosquito larvae each summer. I captured enough fish for a research team seeking to identify the chemical process by which the fish survives the winter freeze. I also captured more than 250 fish, enough for my study to identify their habitat, life size, weight, and foods. My report merited publication and thesis acceptance.

But more than that, I came back home with an understanding of the Arctic. First, at that time, 99% of the Arctic Ocean was covered with a year-round 11-foot blanket of sea ice. Now (2023 A.D.), only about half of the ocean has an ice cover in summertime. And the sea ice that is there measures only 6-feet thick. And the second bit of knowledge came from the land north of the Brooks Range, frozen for centuries. I saw it stretched for miles, deep-frozen with summer cover of arctic grass. In 1955, summer's dead grass never had enough warmth/ time for complete decay. Now in 2023, much warmer than 1955, it does decay, giving off carbon dioxide and methane in great amounts.

Lesson: World climate definitely is getting warmer. We need to adapt to it.

Love,
John

LETTER 20

Dr. Herbert Hanson Guides Me in Master's Degree and Doctorate

Dear Emma,

Through all phases of graduate study, Dr. Herbert Hanson stood at my elbow as my "major professor." He approved my courses and guided my research for both master's and doctoral theses. During my six years at Catholic University, we also became friends. I treasure his memory. A very kind man.

Almost immediately after the final writing of my master's thesis, I started looking for the theme of a doctoral thesis. First, the Navy had no interest in continuing ecological research on the Alaskan blackfish. Second, the Provincial wanted me to focus on animals, not plants. Third, after six months of planning and field work, my attempts to trap and inspect field mice for ectoparasites evaporated. Trapping failed!

So, I settled on what I could find in the sod: "springtails." The CU Biology chairman, an advisor in my research, was surprised that I recognized these very tiny and wingless soil insects. He recommended that I study them, especially since only a very few scientists had bothered to do so. And in DC, there was a lab/library devoted exclusively to the world literature and museum storage of some of the 2,000 species of springtails from all over the world. The lady tech person in charge shared springtail literature with me. I spent three years studying the ecology of springtails, and on the side, discovered two new species. Success!

Lesson: If at first you don't succeed, try something else.

Love,
John

LETTER 21

A Dying Soldier Sparks My Life

Dear Emma,

Yes, a 20-year-old dying soldier handed me a lifetime boost.

It all happened during the morning hours of May 17, 1960, in Washington, DC. On my "to-do" calendar that date? My final doctoral oral exam conducted by the biology faculty at Catholic University at 11:00 a.m. Failure meant? Rank as a full professor … out of reach… ever. I worried but chose to honor my usual morning dawn patrol (5:30-8:00 a.m.) of auxiliary chaplain's duties at Walter Reed Army Hospital. I had found balance in my life by both biology research/study on the one hand and a chaplain's care of sick on the other hand.

Then, the morning happened—like a sledgehammer!

A few minutes before 8:00 a.m., I had just completed my usual rounds at Walter Reed Hospital when a "stat" call came. Catholic chaplain needed immediately! I hurried to it, met the charge nurse, Maj. Dorothy, who I knew well, and questioned her about the case as we hurried to the patient's room. The patient: A 20-year-old enlisted man had attempted to get out of his cot-like bed, slipped, and fell hard against the steel L-shaped bed frame, fracturing both the bones and the nerve cord at the top of the spine, just below the skull. Serious. In fact, VERY SERIOUS.

My question to Dorothy, *"Prognosis?"*

"Zero."

"Has anyone talked to him?"

"No. You are it."

I stopped. *"Dorothy. You mean that?"*

"Yes. You are it."

I took a deep breath. How do I help a 20-year-old meet God today in death? **Lord, help me!**

At his bedside, I first administered essential versions of the sacraments of absolution and anointing of the sick.

But then, I had to be the "it." I must help him realize the serious effects of his fall and assist him to prepare to meet God face-to-face. I started by assuring him that a complete medical team was hurrying to administer their utmost in medical care. But would it be enough? Then for about 10 minutes I spoke of God's concern, how God would help him with a love only God could give. God forgives. God shares mercy. God loves you. The soldier listened. Finally, I left, giving way to the medical team.

Walking back to the nurses' station with Dorothy, I explained my concern and fear of the doctoral oral exam, scheduled for 11:00 a.m. that morning. I concluded, *"This soldier also faces a 'final exam' today, with God as questioner. A bunch of human professors will do that to me. I like my situation much, much better than the dying soldier's!"*

The immense difference between the two "exams" impressed me at my very core. If I failed, I could still be a pastor, itinerant preacher, writer, or… but the dying soldier? Just loving or not loving God in eternal life.

Fast forward to my doctoral oral exam in the biology's conference room at Catholic University, with the clock ticking 11:00 a.m. My fear faded completely! A very strong confidence replaced it! I was charged, and I mean, **charged!** Nothing—the setting, importance, broad subject, prestige of professors—**nothing and no one to fear!** I had just come from helping a young soldier face death! I gave immediate, sure, precise answers to the professors' questions. Nothing fazed me. My voice sure, and I admit, a bit loud.

Toward the end of the hour, the professors realized I had won the day. So, they asked "gimme" questions. One explained that a bush in his backyard had some dead, brown leaves (in May, mind you!) and asked me what he should do. *"Call in a specialist,"* I suggested. Another: *"If the moon is made of green cheese, how did it get it?"* I laughed. The exam had turned to humor. Good sign!

In about an hour, the dean-chairman terminated the exam. I left the room and waited for their verdict. Very shortly, Dr. Herbert Hanson, my respected major professor for six years, came to me with an official, *"You passed very nicely."* But also, with deep concern, he inquired, *"Tell me, what happened to you this morning?"*

From our years of private "cup-of-coffee" discussions, he suspected something very serious shadowed my morning that day. Detail by detail, I related the story about the dying soldier. Dr. Hanson listened intently, and wondered, *"How could you then come to this exam?"*

"That's what we priests may have to do sometimes." The only answer I could think of at that moment.

Now, more than 60 years later, as a retired emeritus professor of biology, I realize that "do-or-die" situations can threaten parents, police, firefighters, etc. Emma, if ever you face tragedy, I pray that God help you, too!

Given the military situation of this, my "war story," and despite my chaplain's rank, I stand at attention and salute you, that young, enlisted soldier, who energized my doctoral exam—and my life in God's service. May you share God's love forever!

Love,
John

LETTER 22

From Assistant Professor to Emeritus

Dear Emma,

Once finished with graduate studies at Catholic University, I moved to my new assignment: the faculty of Quincy College (now University) in June 1960, and residence at its friary. I began as assistant professor of biology and eventually rose to the rank of full professor. Finally, I became emeritus professor, with an honorary degree: LL.D. (Dr. of Laws) and membership in the Athletic Hall of Fame (as a Senior Olympics bowler, I won 36 medals). I also served as vice president for matters of the QU Board of Trustees. I chaired another committee that designed a new community college, which enrolled its students in courses at existing private college-level institutions. It was a new configuration that attracted national attention.

Off campus, the mayor of Quincy appointed me to the city's Public Works Commission during the 1970s. Its members selected me to function as their chairman. I also served on two medical organizations and was invited to speak on ecological subjects. The Illinois government asked me to chair a hearing to select the route for a new highway, I-35.

Lesson: Join community efforts that fit your talents, interests, and background. Avoid both overwork and underwork.

Love.
John

LETTER 23

The Quincy College Researcher

Dear Emma,

Quincy, Illinois, sits on the eastern bluff of the Upper Mississippi River. From the time of its founding in the early 1800s, Quincy became a port for river traffic. And still today, barge after barge fully loaded with grain (especially, soybeans and corn) destined for shipment from New Orleans to foreign countries travel down this mighty river.

To transport grain southward, loaded barges need the river's channel to run at least 9-feet deep. Left to itself, especially during dry seasons, the Upper Mississippi River can't do that. So, a series of about 20 locks and dams from the Twin Cities, Minnesota to Alton, Illinois maintain that depth. In effect, that stretch of the Upper Mississippi River forms a series of lakes, which in turn changes the biological populations and ecology of the river.

In about 1965, Quincy College's Biology Department secured a 27-feet flat-bottom houseboat named the "QC RESEARCHER." It served as a platform for river research equipment and working space for on-site research. Nicely equipped, we offered our services to the Army Corps of Engineers, the federal government's overseers of the Mississippi River. They requested and supported several research projects. Professors Al Pogge, George Schneider, and I, with the help of biology students, succeeded in completing those research requests.

Lesson: Deal with what is at hand, and you can do useful work.

Love.
John

LETTER 24

Higher Education Deepens and Expands

Dear Emma,

The atomic bomb, a giant destroyer of life and city in 1945, opened new roads for higher education to explore. How can we convert the new atomic bomb into "helping" rather than "destroying"? That's the aim, not just for harnessing nuclear power, but also for it to lend a helping hand.

It worked this way for us—in the years 1945-1972—at Quincy College. After the end of World War II, enrollment jumped from approximately 200 students to about 900, when veterans took advantage of government support. Then the "Baby Boomers," born shortly after WWII, boosted student enrollment to nearly 2,000 students by the late 1960s. That's the numbers.

Now, about their education. Most professions also expanded into new issues. Social problems increased.

Communications found quick and immediate ways for people to contact each other. Travel speeded up. New medicines offered cures. Etcetera. In a word, life required quicker decisions with a basketful of new tools—all of which influenced education. How should we educate students to meet this faster, broader way of life?

I offered a first step in an article. Help the student find a fitting niche. Does he/she want to discover a new idea? Or anchor it into a workable plan? Or recruit/train personnel? Or just be a line worker in the plan?

Which fits you? I like Michele Robertson's advice. Avoid both *"sorrow/despair and blind optimism.... Choose hope based on positive vision.... Do what you can. And link up with others."*

Love,
John

LETTER 25

Modernized Communications

Dear Emma,

The 1960s to 2000s saw the rapid and complete change in communications when computers and computer networks became universal. A general pattern that asked help from higher education. In the late 1960s, Quincy College joined a group of Illinois institutions based in another Chicago institution that operated a full, clumsy computer. At first, we sent and received messages by wire. I was one of the faculty members who initiated computer use after an introductory summer course in Chicago. Once started, computers and computer systems grew rapidly and brought significant changes into academic life. How? Printed books? Library? Only when necessary. Pocket-sized electronics could give students and faculty immediate articles.

But old books still rank as treasures. Quincy University's collection of 42 books printed in the years 1450-1500, the birth of printing, still stands as honored "rare books." One-half of them remain the only known copies in the world. In the 1880s, German missionaries quietly transferred them to their American missions to avoid Bismarck's intent to grab and sell them. Today, those rare books live in the Quincy University Library, which is fairly high on the list of libraries with "incunabula," or books, pamphlets and newspapers printed in the earliest stages of printing in Europe.

Lesson: Treasure the wise words of the past. They point to the road for us to follow.

Love,
John

LETTER 26

A Freestanding Quincy College

Dear Emma,

In the late 1960s, like so many other Catholic colleges, Quincy College changed its ownership format. For more than 100 years previous (1860-1960s), the Franciscans owned the college and operated it as a "ministry." All the while, QC paid for the friars' living expenses as one of the many items in its budget.

The reduction in friars and increased number of non-friars on staff and faculty pointed to the need for change. The college president asked me to chair a special committee to explore how best to do so. A brilliant, willing specialist in educational law gave us immense help. He successfully walked us through a complicated process. In the end, Quincy College became a freestanding institution under the Catholic/Franciscan flag, governed by a board of trustees. Now, 50 years later, as Quincy University, that flag still flies with dignity.

The new pattern of ownership also changed the status of the friars on staff from an ownership role to that of employees, standing side-by-side with non-friars on staff/faculty. In turn, for the first time, we friars could enroll in a retirement plan. I chose the TIAA-CREF, a nationwide program for college professors. Very happy that I did! It works!

Lesson: Sometimes we need to change things. Seek advice. Plan together. Choose a workable path that helps people.

Love,
John

LETTER 27

Quincy College Has a "Baby Brother"

Dear Emma,

"Baby brother?" Well… sorta. You see, in the early 1970s, Illinois decided to divide the entire state into community college districts and to erect an active "junior college" in each district. Quincy College became the anchor site of a three-county community-college district. That set off alarms at QC.

QC President Fr. Titus Ludes, OFM, asked me to head a committee addressing the new situation. I turned to the same educational lawyer who we had used in the ownership change process. And he rang the winner's bell…LOUDLY! Here's how he did it:

If another district could legally ask a private college to teach a music course to its community college students, then we here in the new community college district ought to be in legal conformity by asking that our new community college enroll all of its students in existing private, post-high school institutions. A wonderful answer! It passed legal scrutiny! And nationally, QC's plan received a pat on the back when the United States Congress invited the Quincy College academic dean to address them in session.

To assist our champion lawyer, I invited high school students in our district to state their curriculum hopes. That information told us that we could meet their desires in all fields except agriculture. Then I sought help from other private, post-high school institutions located in the new district. They smiled and joined us. Result? The new John Woods Community College became a reality through community effort, with Quincy College as both organizer and professor.

Lesson: Unite! Work/Play/Plan together for a common good.

Love,
John

LETTER 28

"How Much to Get This Job?"

Dear Emma,

One time a man asked me that question. Seriously! One I never expected. It happened this way: In the early 1970s, Quincy's mayor invited me, an ecologist, to join a group of prominent citizens to form a special city public works committee. The members elected me as chairman.

The city's old sewage disposal plant could not meet new standards. So, the city decided to replace it. We visited new plants in other cities and talked with state and national officials to seek the best modern way to treat waste. Next, we searched for an experienced architect/designer/construction supervisor. We narrowed the number of replies to about six.

Then one day, without an appointment, an owner/president at one of the select companies came to my office at Quincy College. He expressed strong interest in designing this new sewage plant and complimented me on my apparent influence in the city. I kept quiet. But then he asked, *"How much does it take for me to get this job?"* Bribe? He's offering me—a priest, a professor—a bribe! I replied in measured and very terse terms, *"I will use my influence to see that you do not get this job or any other job in this city!"* He stood and replied, *"I oversold myself,"* and left.

Later, the committee backed me. Not even one vote for him.

Lesson: Some people do bad things. Choose the right way.

Love,
John

LETTER 29

Leaving Teaching and Joining Retreat Ministry

Dear Emma,

In the summer of 1983, I left teaching. The Franciscan Provincial assigned me to the retreat ministry at our retreat center in Indianapolis. I liked that appointment! I could now delve more deeply into study of the gospels especially. And I could be more truly living the injunction St. Francis of Assisi spelled out in the first sentence of his Rule for us Franciscans: *"The rule and life of the Friars Minor is this, namely, to observe the Holy Gospel of our Lord, Jesus Christ…."*

And I could help retreatants reach a deeper love of Jesus. One such instance: The leader of a non-Catholic, Christian group asked to spend a weekend retreat with us because, as he said, *"We know the gospels, but not how to pray them. You at the retreat center can help us because you pray."*

To start them off, I explained one way of praying a gospel story. First, imagine that you were one of the bystanders in a gospel incident, then ask Jesus a question, or compliment him, or make a comment. Praying implies a conversation with God. In appreciation, the leader of that group presented to me a "shadow" carving of the birth of Jesus.

Lesson: Prayer is conversation with God. Speak to God. Listen to God.

Love,
John

LETTER 30

Marriage Preparation Retreats

Dear Emma,

One of the most successful programs conducted at our Indianapolis retreat center featured a time of prayer and reflection on marriage. Engaged couples attended this weekend as preparation for their upcoming life together. Fr. Martin Wolter, OFM, designed and conducted it once a month. It was a program that was always crowded.

One instance affirmed the correctness of the program. One young lady informed us that she and her boyfriend saw unsolved and important differences between them and decided to cancel their future marriage. A year or two later, she returned with a different boyfriend. That one worked.

Another successful retreat, designed and conducted by Fr. Justin Belitz, OFM, emphasized good foundational life features, religion included. Today, nearly 50 years later, Fr. Justin still carries on.

Lesson: Find programs that appeal to and work for you.

Love,
John

LETTER 31

Itinerant Preacher

Dear Emma,

Later, after serving as administrator of the Indianapolis retreat center, I became an "itinerant retreat master." I traveled all over the USA, mostly by car with some by air or rail, giving retreats, Forty Hours, and special lectures at parishes, convents, and retreat centers.

I tried to fit words, messages, and encouragement to the specific listeners in each place I led retreats. Here's how it once brought me a broad smile: Place: A nun's convent. Event: Retreat for elderly, retired nuns (a couple dozen or so of them). I don't remember the exact subject of my talk, but I pointed out something that they could do, even in their advanced retirement years. After that lecture. One of the nuns came up to me with a broad smile, thanking me for *"giving them something to do."* In all honesty, I don't remember at all what that *"something"* was.

Lesson: Meet other peoples' needs as close as you can.

Love,
John

LETTER 32

Ministry as a Part-Time Hospital Chaplain

Dear Emma,

I offered to change addresses and ministries several times. When the need arose for a part-time Franciscan hospital chaplain, I volunteered. I had taught prospective doctors, lab personnel and nurses. Now, late in life, I could join them in actual care.

Direct care offered a surprise here and there. Even two, on one day! In a big general hospital in central Memphis, Tennessee, I answered a call about an elderly, Catholic woman in coma who was near death. At her bedside, with her family present, I administered the Sacrament of the Sick. When I anointed her forehead, she opened her eyes and watched me, clear as a bell, and then closed them when I finished the anointing. Her family noted that moment of clarity.

Afterwards, as I walked down the hospital corridor, a 30(ish)-year-old man standing at a patient's door stopped me and invited me to anoint his comatose Dad, the patient in that room. His brother joined, and a nurse came by to check on the patient. As usual, I bent over, near to the Dad's ear, quietly identified myself, and offered to administer the Sacrament of the Sick. He raised his leg in an effort to answer me. That amazed his sons! As the nurse and I left, we heard the sons apologizing to him for some old incident.

Lesson: God most surely has a sense of humor.

Love,
John

LETTER 33

Some Additional Hospital Incidents

Dear Emma,

In this letter I would like to report on three children, all cancer patients in St. Jude's Children Hospital, Memphis, Tennessee. During the 1990s, I served as part-time Catholic chaplain at the famous hospital that actor Danny Thomas founded and funded. Three cases of note, as I remember them:

First one: Girl, about 12-13 years old from Chile, South America, with advanced, stubborn cancer. She was very religious and wanted communion every time I visited. She died. Several months later, her mother found her last Christmas card, which her daughter addressed, *"Dear Jesus, Happy birthday!"*

Second one: Boy, about 10-12 years old, with cancer. I can still see his mother on one side of the bed, talking with a nurse on the other side. Mom was thanking the nurse for the wonderful care given her boy. He remarks, *"Sometimes it works, sometimes it doesn't."* Two weeks later, he died. He, the realist.

Third one: Baby girl, about nine months old. She had been in the hospital for about six months, fighting the disease. I mean, really fighting hard and noticeably so. Something I had never seen before or after. Some babies can really fight! She died.

My thought? Someday, I hope to meet all three of them in heaven. Are you with me on that?

Love,
John

LETTER 34

Published Articles

Dear Emma,

In the late 1980s, I began publishing short articles in the Diocesan papers of the various dioceses in which I lived. All of them without pay, but as contributions. One series featured commentary on the Sunday gospels. Another, a series of letters called **"Dear Jesus."** And finally, a very long series under the title, **"Whispers of God."** Each article was rarely over 100 words. My reason: Keep them short and people will read the entire article.

I never kept an accurate count but I estimate that about 400 to 500 were published. An interested reader can contact the Franciscan archivist. Routinely, I sent a copy of each published article to the archivist of OFM at St. Anthony Friary in St. Louis, Missouri.

This letter ends the series on various personal incidents. More could be written but these should provide a peek through the window of my life.

I now plan to offer a summary of my principles/beliefs in the remaining letters.

Love,
John

LETTER 35

The First of These Letters About What Makes Me Tick

Dear Emma,

I hope the previous letters gave you an understanding of *"What I have done."* In this letter and following, I intend to change the theme to: *"Why, I did them that way."* Or, in other words, *"What fundamental beliefs guide my life?"*

Beginning in September 1936, the start of my high school years, I attended Franciscan institutions until priesthood ordination in June 1949. Then I taught nearly 26 years, during which I gained more knowledge of and adherence to an acceptance of Franciscan thinking and life, strengthening a lifelong following in the footsteps of St. Francis of Assisi.

After my teaching career, I began a life-long study, research and writing about how ecology, medicine, and scripture can work together. In turn, this brought me into two major areas of life principles: **Wisdom** and **Love**. Let's look at those two major views of life in the following letters, Emma.

Love,
John

LETTER 36

Wisdom and Love

Dear Emma,

Human life involves a complex core of systems, a fact each person faces. Where we live. What we do. Why we do it, and more. I ask that each of us consider these two core models for our thinking, choosing, and action: **Wisdom** and **Love**.

Wisdom stands as the top step of a "Ladder of Wisdom," which is built on three other steps: 1) **Data**, its bottom step, consists of individual facts; 2) **Information**, a generalization of facts; 3) **Knowledge**, the third step of the ladder, explains and predicts; and 4) **Wisdom**, the top step of the ladder, contains understanding.

Love merits equality with **Wisdom**. It also can be described as a "Ladder of Love." A baby loves its mother, then father and family, schoolmates, city, country, and the whole human race.

By itself, neither **Wisdom** nor **Love** can describe the totality of human life. Combined, they can. We need both to work together. In my estimation, each of us should attempt to find a satisfactory merging of wisdom and love in our lives.

And, secondly, I hope that each person recognizes God as the final step in both "ladders." A personal God, not just a written law. There's where we find both, ultimate **Wisdom** and **Love**.

Love,
John

LETTER 37

Wisdom and Love Inside God

Dear Emma,

Yes, indeed, Wisdom and Love both reside in God and act in absolute harmony. To start with: We believe that the Three Divine Persons—Father, Son and Holy Spirit—live with each other in such completely intense harmony and love that together they form One God.

Further, we also believe that the Three Persons always lived and will continue to live without ever ending.

We also believe that the love within the Three Persons satisfies them completely. God absolutely has no need to create us but does so out of love.

The Three Persons simply want to share love with us humans.

Where does God stand in the ladders of Wisdom and Love?

My response: God stands as the top ring in both ladders. God does so as a person, not just a lawgiver. God IS the law.

God loves you, Emma.

Love,
John

LETTER 38

God Reaches Out to Every Person All the Time

Dear Emma,

Over 12 to 13 billion years ago, God first created a place for us humans to live: The cosmos with the globe called Earth. A viable, beautiful, and livable home for humans. Then, some 2,000 years ago, as the *"Wisdom Ladder"* demonstrates and the *"Love Ladder"* affirms, God sent Jesus as a hinge connecting God with humans. Jesus, both God and human wrapped into one, came to help God reach out to us, and we to respond in kind to God.

Jesus himself points out that, *"I am the way and the truth and the life. No one comes to the Father except through me. If you know* ***me****, then you will also know my Father."* (John 14:6-7). *"Truth"* and *"Life"* qualify *"way."*

Jesus establishes his direct authority to God. He also announces that he will convey our messages to God.

Jesus also laid out a telling summary of what God wants us to do: *"You shall love the Lord, your God with all your* ***heart, soul, and mind****...and your neighbor as yourself."* (Matthew 22:36-39).

And finally, Jesus asks, *"Father... I wish that where I am, they [true believers] may be with me."* (John 17:24). He promises Heaven to humans who respond in love to God.

Love,
John

LETTER 39

Love of Neighbor

Dear Emma,

At every moment of every day, God invites us to love our "neighbor." In short, I understand that to mean: When I love God, I also love everyone whom God loves. I want for everyone what God wants for them. I can't "like" everyone, but I can want for every person I meet what God wants for that person.

To "love neighbor," in my understanding, also includes the environment. Humans need a healthy surrounding for good living. God provides that. Let's not spoil it.

Loving neighbor, I think, includes loving nature. I hope you have a place for living in an environment that provides for your needs and comfort.

Love,
John

LETTER 40

End of Life, Entry to Afterlife

Dear Emma,

One thing is for sure: Life here on Earth will eventually end for us. Then, we enter afterlife, a life which has no ending. We call that moment death.

During life before death, we prepare for life after death. Before death, we have bodies and things in time and space but no direct face-to-face contact with God.

In the moment of death, we leave body, things, time, and space, and enter face-to-face contact with God, who asks, *"Do you love me?"* For the person who replies, *"Yes,"* that's Heaven. For the person who answers, *"No,"* that's Hell. Both Heaven and Hell are unending actions.

With this letter, I bring this personal autobiography to a close.

Above all, may the Good Lord be with you at every step in your life!

Bless! Love!
John

Made in the USA
Monee, IL
14 July 2023